Contents

Acknowledgements

This handbook bears testament to the expertise, support and dedication of a range of colleagues and students from across the University who pursue the attainment of a truly inclusive learning and teaching environment.

It could not have been achieved without them and we wish to express our gratitude to:

Claire Allam
Gary Albutt
Ryan Armitage
Kathryn Axon
John Barrett
Andrea Bath
Simon Beecroft
Gareth Braid
Tom Bramall
Henry Brunskill
April Dawson
Sue Davison
Alex Erdlenburgh
Angharad Evans
Marie Evans
Kevin Farnsworth
Chris Firth
David Forrest
Deborah Fowler
Angela Gascoyne
James Goldingay
Jackie Gresham
Alison Griffin
Katherine Harrell
Jennifer Hastings
Ali Hayward
Tim Herrick
Chris Ince
Sajeev Jeganathan
Glynis Jones
Bob Johnston
Plato Kapranos
Richard Kelwick
Terry Lamb
Mark Limb
James Little
Angela Marron
Graham McElearney
Danny Monaghan
Michelle Moore
David Mowbray
Marika Panayiotou
Anne Peat
Alan Phillips
David Phillips
Adrian Powell
Tom Rhodes
Elena Rodriguez-Falcon
Anthony Rossiter
Jenny Rowson
Emily Savage
Carolyn Shelbourn
Sharah Shreeve
Jane Spooner
Patsy Stark
Brendan Stone
Juliet Storey
Anna Symington
Holly Taylor
Katrin Thomson
Rebecca Watson
Darren Webb
Paul White
Wendy Whitehouse
Louise Woodcock

… and all the other students and staff who, by sharing their experience, influenced and supported this project.

Background

The Inclusive Learning and Teaching (ILT) Project was launched in 2007 as one of the strategic learning and teaching priorities of the University of Sheffield.

The distinctive approach of the Project was its scope, which was not limited to working with specific groups of students, such as disabled students, but which had a vision of:

'A University of Sheffield learning culture which enables ***all our students*** from whatever background to achieve their full potential'.

During the life of the project over 500 students were consulted; over 400 staff engaged in debates and conversations; over 1500 academic staff and teachers received 'hints and tips' for inclusive practice from students and 11 academic departments ran specific ILT projects.

This handbook is the culmination of this work. Many people, staff and students, took part and we would like to share some of what we have learned with you. The enthusiasm and positive engagement of students has informed and directed much of our activity, it has also demonstrated that raising our awareness of inclusive learning and teaching and making changes to our practice can help students make the best of their time at university and support them in becoming independent learners and critical thinkers. Moreover, the active participation of students in their learning helps build a sense of identity and community that further empowers them.

The Inclusive Learning and Teaching Handbook will help you to get involved. We hope you will find it both useful and inspiring, a resource that can be dipped into rather than read from front to back.

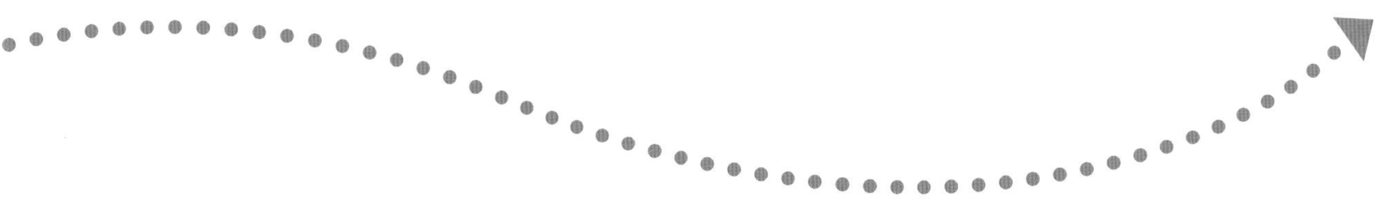

Why you should read this handbook: Introduction

At a time when the world faces one of the most severe financial challenges ever, climate change threatens mankind in different ways, and lack of resources begin to affect our life styles, we turn for solutions to our governments, research organisations and education institutions. But are these organisations ready to take on the challenges? Are we able to keep up with the pace at which these challenges are occurring? Do we have the capabilities to generate solutions, produce capable and adaptable professionals to deal with these threats?

In higher education institutions we have the academic capabilities to develop ideas and generate solutions through our research. Researchers and scientists battle with the problems of this era on a day-to-day basis, seeking innovative applications of current and emerging technology, discovering new treatments for illnesses, finding alternative methods to generate energy, or even establishing new approaches for wealth generation and job creation.

All of this, however, requires a sound intellectual education that challenges convention and promotes innovation and creativity. All of this needs people to undertake the challenges – people from different backgrounds, ideals, beliefs, abilities and ways of thinking. It requires an inclusive learning, teaching and research attitude and culture to enable students, staff and stakeholders to develop their full potential and ultimately contribute to the challenges of this day.

Being inclusive within this context also requires understanding, preparedness and resources to enable us to deal with an increasingly diverse set of student backgrounds, ability and attainment and larger classes whilst endeavouring to provide an excellent learning experience. All done at a time when public expenditure means resources are to be spread more thinly! So what to do?

This handbook aims to address this issue by providing its reader with some ideas and examples of practical steps that easily can be taken to minimise the barriers to learning and increase participation of our students in their education. First, however, we need to understand what we mean by 'inclusive learning and teaching' as it can be a somewhat nebulous concept. Working within education, teaching and learning are familiar terms. On its own 'inclusion' is easily understood. When you combine them together and create the concept of 'inclusive learning and teaching' it is much harder to define. This is because there is no single definition, its meaning is dependent on the specific nature of a situation – practice which includes one person/student may exclude another. The only constant is its purpose: that all are able to achieve.

This is a bold aspiration but the material in this handbook also highlights the key factors, identified by the University of Sheffield's Inclusive Learning and Teaching Project, which ensure that all students are able to achieve and contribute to a future that is happy and secure, both for themselves and for future generations. An ideal that we can, and must, all subscribe to.

Releasing new concepts

Hints and tips for inclusive learning and teaching

Here, practical advice and suggestions combine to provide a collection of pointers that are designed to encourage a 'small steps' approach to inclusive learning and teaching. Be it creating effective presentations; designing assessments, or utilising new technologies in teaching, there is a wealth of advice, drawn from students' experiences, to help you.

For further information go to:
www.sheffield.ac.uk/lets/projects/inclusivel&t/hintsandtips.html

The hints and tips overview

Glossary

The majority of our readers will be from the University of Sheffield. For those who are not, the following may be helpful:

MOLE (My Online Learning Environment) is the University's virtual learning environment.

MUSE (My University of Sheffield Environment) is a portal giving access to the University's online resources.

uSpace: an online collaborative environment provided by the University of Sheffield.

TASH (The Academic Skills Hub) resources for skills development: www.tash.group.shef.ac.uk

LeTS (Learning and Teaching Services): www.sheffield.ac.uk/lets

CICS (Corporate Information and Computing Services): www.sheffield.ac.uk/cics

Make your office hours clear

Simple steps for effective interaction with students

Name: Rita

We love our personal tutor; don't be afraid to let us know who you are!

Our tutors and lecturers are a great source of help. Please make clear to us your office hours so that we know when best to contact you.

- Keep your online university profile up to date so that students can find your contact details easily.
- Make information available to students about when it is best to contact you (e.g. your office hours).
- Understand the make-up of your student body, and think about how you can support their diverse needs. Good sources of information are: the student enquiry system (via MUSE), your departmental secretary, your departmental disability liaison officer, teaching international students resources at: www.sheffield.ac.uk/lets/thinkglobal
- When you first meet your students, introduce yourself, talk about your research interests, make it clear how you want to be addressed and explain how your role as lecturer or personal tutor supports their learning.
- The winners of the "I love my Personal Tutor" campaign (an initiative from the Students' Union) all took a little time to "value the needs of students." Try to get to know your students a little better.
- Explain clearly and make available to students information about your tutorial system.

serif
removal

Producing accessible handouts

Name: Derek

If you provide notes (online or hard copy) before classes it makes your lecture more accessible to all your students.

Please give handouts that are clear and highly visible.

Please tell us the different types of assessment you will be using.

Planning:

- **Releasing handouts at the start of a module** gives students time to prepare and think critically about the subject material and can increase student engagement in the lecture.
- Think about **different ways you might display the information** in your handouts. A picture, chart or table may be more powerful than a paragraph of text.
- Producing a handout at the start that details the **different types of assessment** you will be using will help all students to see what is expected of them and highlight areas of study skills support they may need early on.

When designing handouts ask yourself:

- Have I used an accessible font such Arial, Tahoma, Futura or another sans-serif font so that the text is clearly defined and spaced?
- Is the font size 12+ for printed handouts and 28+ for presentations?
- Have I used a font colour that is highly visible and contrasts with the background?
- Have I moved text away from underlying background images, patterns or textures?
- Have I aligned the text to the left, rather than justified it, so that it is easier to read?
- For more information, have a look at Techdis's excellent Accessibility Essentials guides covering Word, PowerPoint and more: www.techdis.ac.uk

Print-outs:

- If your document needs to be printed on coloured paper, choose light blue, cream or yellow rather than green, pink or red, which are less accessible for dyslexic readers.
- If printing double-sided (which saves paper) use decent quality paper to minimise print showing on the other side.

Publish online:

- Putting handouts online through MOLE allows the integration of accessibility features and gives students 24/7 flexible access to learning content and lets students read at their own pace. This is especially helpful to international, mature and disabled students.

critical
Thinking
DO NOT
EXCEED
DOSAGE

Introducing critical thinking to students

Name: Nicole

Please explain what critical thinking is, and break us in gently!

Please point us in the direction of study skills support.

Critical thinking

Critical thinking is a way to explore and discover the underpinning meaning or implications of ideas, concepts and discipline specific knowledge. Developing critical thinking skills equips students with the ability to draw out more reasoned arguments and understand the wider implications of their knowledge.

When thinking about critical thinking:

- Consider the many definitions of critical thinking. Some are more accessible and relevant to a particular discipline than others.
- Introduce critical thinking into assessment and teaching exercises gradually over the semester, perhaps as early as year one.
- Help students by explaining simple approaches to critical thinking e.g. **P.E.E**
  - **P**oint (make a point, statement or suggest an idea about the subject material).
  - **E**xplain (explain your point, idea or statement).
  - **E**vidence (reinforce your point with theoretical knowledge or examples from the subject material).
- Highlight to students the critical thinking elements of assessments at the start of a module. This will give students time to consider their critical thinking skills and whether they may need to access study skills support.

TASH (The Academic Skills Hub) has a section on critical thinking with links to more resources: www.tash.group.shef.ac.uk

Smile!

Understanding individual needs

Name: Rajiv

Smile! It makes it easier for us to approach you and explain how our disability might affect the way we learn.

Please don't make assumptions. Two students with dyslexia might have different needs.

The University of Sheffield welcomes students from all sectors of society, creating a vibrant learning environment filled with differing expectations and diverse student needs. Approximately 6.5% of students at this University have declared a disability, that's around 1,700 students.

What kinds of support might students need?

- Students may need extra help with studying. Look at: www.sheffield.ac.uk/lets/projects/inclusivel&t/support_for_students.html
- The Disability and Dyslexia Support Service has produced the 'DDSS Handbook' which is also an excellent example of accessible design. Downloadable from: www.sheffield.ac.uk/disability

How to identify support needs

- Try to get to know your students a little better; it will help you to identify particular needs. See 'Simple steps for effective interaction with students' (page 9 for advice.
- Be aware that students may have multiple support needs and not all disabilities may be 'visible'.
- Your departmental disability liaison officer (DLO) will be able to give you advice about identifying and meeting your students' support needs.

How to meet the needs of students

- Design handouts and presentations to be as accessible as possible – look at other hints and tips such as 'Producing accessible handouts' (page 11).
- Think about the international dimensions to your course: www.sheffield.ac.uk/lets/thinkglobal
- Become familiar with reasonable adjustments to examinations and assessments. Examples of common reasonable adjustments are given below:
  - Flexible examination timetabling.
  - Additional time in examination and rest breaks (typically 15 minutes extra for dyslexic students).
  - Allowing students to use a computer in examinations, for spell checker and dictation software.
  - The use of an amanuensis (scribe).

Where to go for more information

- A copy of 'Supporting our Students – A Guide' can be requested from the Student Services Information Desk: www.sheffield.ac.uk/ssid
- Disability & Dyslexia Support Service: www.sheffield.ac.uk/disability
- English Language Teaching Centre: www.sheffield.ac.uk/eltc
- The Open University provides guidance on meeting the needs of students: www.open.ac.uk/inclusiveteaching

Presentations that work

Name: Nabila

Please make presentations visible to all by following basic presentation guidelines.

OHP's can be an excellent alternative to Power Point in some lectures, but only if the transparencies are really clear and there are some relevant notes available online.

Designing PowerPoint and overhead projector presentations

- Use a font size of 28+
- Use an accessible font such Arial, Tahoma, Futura or another sans-serif font so that the text is easy to read.
- For Overhead Projector (OHP) acetate sheets use large and clear handwriting, or alternatively, printed acetate sheets can be a more accessible option.
- Use a font or pen colour that is highly visible and contrasts distinctively with the background (e.g. black or very dark blue against a white background).
- Make sure that any diagrams, figures or charts are large, readable and clear. Be aware that some diagrams may give less information to red/green colour blind students.
- Keep slides and OHP acetate sheets clear of unnecessary clutter, such as excessive text. Keeping the content of each slide restricted to three main bullet points or one diagram will make it easier for students to follow.
- Consider engaging your audience by integrating accessible multimedia features into your PowerPoint presentations such as sound, video, (animated) diagrams or pictures or by making them into screencasts. Learning and Teaching Services (LeTS) offer information, advice and a space for you to try these technologies: www.sheffield.ac.uk/lets/techno/media/diy-suite.html

For more information, have a look at Techdis's excellent Accessibility Essentials guides covering Word, PowerPoint and more: www.techdis.ac.uk

PowerPoint print-outs and publishing online

- Before printing out remove any slide background colours that make the text difficult to read. This is especially problematic if printing in black and white.
- Ensure that slides are readable – do not print more than six slides per page.
- The font size when printed out should be about size 12 for text.

- Publishing PowerPoint presentations online gives students flexible access to learning content and allows students to use any accessible multimedia features that have been integrated into the presentation.
- Publishing PowerPoint presentations online allows students to read the notes at the bottom of the page, where more detail can be added to the information on the slide.

For more information about accessible handouts (online and offline) see 'Producing accessible handouts' (Page 11).

f

Assessment matters

Name: Lee

Please set hand-in dates as flexibly as possible to avoid clashes.

Please don't make assessment just about exams, we can show our talents in different ways. Please give feedback part-way through the module, not always at the end.

What is a pass mark? International students often have different expectations of what is required to pass.

Accessible assessments

- Be explicit about the methods of assessment you are using. Make it clear to students what will be tested in different types of assessment, and how and why, at the start of the module.
- Explain clearly, perhaps with model answers, what is expected of them.
- Reasonable adjustments can be made to all types of assessment to make them more accessible to students. See our 'Understanding individual needs' (page 15) hints and tips.
- Consider spreading out assessments to minimise periods of intense pressure.
- Using a range of appropriate forms of assessment enables students to expand their ability to think critically and develop a broader skill set. This skill set is a key element of the distinctiveness of the 'Sheffield Graduate': www.sheffield.ac.uk/sheffieldgraduate

Accessible feedback should be:

- Frequent and provided quickly enough to be useful. Make it clear when students can expect to receive feedback. Ideally feedback should be returned early enough for students to identify areas they can improve on for the next assessment and help them to self-correct.
- Focussed on learning rather than marks. It should provide opportunities for students to critically reflect on their progress.
- Linked to the assessment criteria/learning outcomes.
- Understandable. Different forms of feedback can be given, for example, online feedback, a facilitated discussion between lecturers or tutors and students part-way through a module, peer feedback, MP3 recordings etc.

What is a pass mark?

- Students, especially international students, may have had very different previous assessment experiences. For example, they may have had assessments consisting only of taught content exams, routinely achieving marks between 75 and 100. It can also be a shock that a grade of 60 is a good mark! Explain to students that only on rare occasions will they achieve a grade of 75–100 for truly exceptional work. You may want to explore with them what these experiences have been.

Case studies and initiatives

The University has adopted six 'principles of feedback' as standard practice:
www.sheffield.ac.uk/content/1/c6/08/79/71/Principles-of-Feedback.pdf

Case Studies Wiki

The Case Studies Wiki is an exciting collaboration between academics and students. Assessment and feedback issues are explored through real case study examples:
www.good.group.shef.ac.uk/wiki/index.php/Assessment_and_Feedback

TASH (The Academic Skills Hub) has a section on assessment with links to more resources:
www.tash.group.shef.ac.uk

...try a variety of teaching approaches
WHEN OUT OF THE FOREST THERE LOOMED... AN ESSAY DEADLINE!
RARR! ESSAY!!
DEADLINE
ONLY 3 DAYS TO GO!
NEW DEADLINE?
I don't think so!

The inclusive classroom

Name: Sue

Please include a variety of teaching/learning methods in lectures and tutorials.

Please encourage discussions in your class and try to involve all students, it will help you to understand which areas we find difficult.

Do group work for projects and promote integration in groups.

Learning styles

We all learn differently, influenced by the combination of our past educational experiences, study practices and personal approach to specific tasks. This can be described as our learning style, defined as 'particular ways of gathering, processing and storing information and experiences' (Cuthbert, P.F., 2005). It is reasonable to assume that students will perform better in tasks that reflect their particular style of learning, so knowledge of your students' learning styles and including a variety of tasks will make your teaching more inclusive.

Introducing learning styles to students

- At the start of a course explain ideas about learning styles to your students.
- A learning style questionnaire could be handed out at the start of a course to encourage students to explore their own learning style and to inform you about the learning styles of your students.

The ILT website has links and resources including learning style tests:
www.sheffield.ac.uk/lets/projects/inclusivel&t/learningstyles.html

How to address different learning styles

Students learn better when presented with information that is conveyed in a way that best suits their learning style. To address these different learning styles:

- Convey information in different ways e.g. diagrams, speech, text, discussion, practical tasks etc.
- Use multimedia technologies such as videos, podcasts and screencasts in lectures and make them available on MOLE. Learning and Teaching Services (LeTS) offer information, advice and a space for you to try these technologies:
  www.sheffield.ac.uk/lets/techno/media/diy-suite.html

Set activities that enable students with different learning styles to engage and progress such as:

- Encouraging subject-related discussions in small groups or across a lecture theatre. The discussions may also highlight areas students find difficult.
- Formative or summative assessments that promote group work can: create a safe environment for students to integrate and participate, help students get to know each other, build a group – not an audience, allow different styles of contribution to be valued.

Language in lectures

Name: Nadeem

Please get a student or colleague to check how user-friendly your lecture is.

Please don't talk too fast and please use accessible language – explain colloquialisms and acronyms.

Give us a chance to ask questions, we like to show off how interested we are in the subject.

Planning to use accessible language

- Plan how to explain, at the start of a course, the learning objectives in clear and jargon-free language to your students.
- Use clear, unambiguous language for assessments. Consider providing a list of word definitions, see: www.sheffield.ac.uk/lets/projects/internat/resources.html
- Avoid using abbreviations in questions unless they are explained.
- Practice your lecture in front of a colleague to ensure that your lecture is relevant, engaging and uses accessible language. These considerations should also form part of peer observation.

Use good presentation techniques:

- Speak clearly and not too quickly.
- Use clear and concise language.
- Do not use unexplained colloquialisms/slang as international students may not understand them.
- Avoid using acronyms or abbreviations as far as possible. If you have to use acronyms or abbreviations, clearly explain the meaning of them to your students.
- Consider providing a running glossary of terms either in lectures or on MOLE.

Language to 'engage'

- Allocate time at the end of each lecture to allow students to ask questions.
- When a student asks a question across the lecture theatre, repeat the question out loud so that all students can benefit from the question and your answer.

When talking directly to students with mobility aids:

- Do not move their mobility aid (walking stick/frame, wheel chair etc.) without explicit consent from the student. Avoid crouching or leaning over them. Respect their mobility aid and view it as part of the student's personal space.
- If possible talk to students with a mobility aid at their level. Sit down if you must, to maintain eye contact.

English language support for academics and students

The English Language Teaching Centre (ELTC) offers a range of language advice and support services including:

- A writing advisory service to help improve academic writing skills.
- Full and part-time English language courses.
- Dyslexia support.

For more information:

www.sheffield.ac.uk/eltc

Engaging lectures

Name: Elinor

Make lectures a joy by keeping the subject interesting and engaging – use lots of examples.

Make lectures accessible to students of all levels of ability.

Please give us time to write down key information.

"Tell me, and I forget. Show me, and I remember. Involve me, and I understand."
(Chinese proverb)

"Effective teachers: (a) present material in a clear and engaging manner and (b) focus on the interpersonal factors that characterise classrooms and establish rapport with students"
(Goldstein, G.S. & Benassi, V.A., 2006).

Preparing to engage

Reflect on whether your teaching:

- Motivates your students
- Sparks interest
- Creates a learning-friendly environment
- Feeds-back and feeds-forward on progress
- Provides relevant, real-life learning opportunities
- Rewards engagement
- Encourages self-motivation

Inspire and motivate your students

- Explore lecture ideas and concepts in context. Use lots of interesting examples.
- Illustrate the broader relevance and implications of lecture concepts. (A characteristic of 'The Sheffield Graduate' is to understand the wider social, cultural and economic context of their academic knowledge and skills-base).
- Pace your lecture so that all students have time to write down important notes.
- Avoid showing negativity towards difficult concepts. If appropriate, use humour.
- Break up lectures by introducing Q&A (question and answer) or short 'partner-work' sessions; use an electronic group response system: www.sheffield.ac.uk/lets/techno/services/egrs.html
- Consider the existing knowledge needed for your lecture and explain this to your students at the start. This will allow students of all levels of ability to identify areas of background knowledge that they need to focus on.
- Allocate time in your lecture to allow students to discuss or ask questions about the ideas, topics and concepts raised.

For 101 tips on how to engage students:

www.smartteaching.org/blog/2008/08/100-motivational-techniques-to-take-learning-to-the-next-level

For ideas about the qualities possessed by engaging lecturers read:

Goldstein, G.S. & Benassi, V.A. (2006) Students' and Instructors' Beliefs about Excellent Lecturers and Discussion Leaders. *Research in Higher Education* 46, 685–707.

j

Making online materials more accessible

Name: Daniel

We would like to connect to our study materials 24/7, anywhere in the world. Using MUSE and MOLE can make this happen.

Online resources help those of us who cannot easily access the library. Online learning really benefits students with disabilities, mature and international students.

What can I publish online?

- Handouts: see 'Producing accessible handouts' (page 11) for more information.
- PowerPoint presentations.
- Screen-casts (automated presentations with audio narration).
- Guided web-based tutorials.
- Videos and podcasts.
- Links to carefully selected websites.
- Interactive content and features that enable students to share their learning experience:
  - Create discussion groups.
  - Create a blog and allow students to post entries.

Where can I publish online?

- You could create your own website or blog:
  www.blogger.com
  www.webs.com
- The safest method of publishing online is on an intranet, e.g. MUSE/MOLE/uSpace at the University of Sheffield.

Which students benefit from online content?

- All students benefit from 24/7 worldwide access to learning resources.
- Accessibility features such as screen-readers make online content much more accessible. This is of great help in removing barriers to learning for dyslexic and disabled students. See: www.skillsforaccess.org.uk/index.php
- International students may spend periods of time in their home countries. Access to online resources provides the flexibility to work from anywhere.
- Mature, international and disabled students may not always have easy access to the library. Online delivery gives students flexible access to library and course resources where ever they are.

Who can help me design and publish online content?

Learning and Teaching Services (LeTS) offer information, advice and a space for you to try a range of multimedia technologies. See: www.sheffield.ac.uk/lets/techno/media/diy-suite.html

Corporate Information and Computing Services (CiCS) offer support on how to use and publish online content using MUSE/MOLE:

- For more information about MOLE: www.sheffield.ac.uk/mole/news.html
- For more information about MUSE: www.sheffield.ac.uk/cics/muse

The Student Services Department has produced guidelines about designing student friendly online content: www.sheffield.ac.uk/ssd/web/design.html

Planning your teaching

Name: Melanie

Please communicate with other staff teaching on your module so you give us consistent messages.

Please use available technology, to add some variety.

Have you ever used video or audio in your lectures? Some students learn better that way.

Accessible from the start – inclusive by design

"Great oaks from little acorns grow". Small changes made at the planning stage have a significant effect on removing barriers to learning for all students.

Simple steps to accessible planning

1. Designing the course framework

- Think about the learning objectives of your course. Do your learning objectives represent what you would like your students to gain from your course? Can students with different learning styles meet those learning objectives?
- What skills will your course help students to develop? Are those skills important in developing 'The Sheffield Graduate'? www.sheffield.ac.uk/sheffieldgraduate

2. Think about your students

- What background knowledge do you expect your students to have? Think about the support services and resources you can recommend to students that don't have the specific pre-requisite knowledge you have in mind. Can you make your teaching more flexible to adapt to changing student needs?

3. Designing course content

- Do your PowerPoint, OHP slides and handouts follow basic accessibility guidelines?
- Have you considered how to make your learning content more accessible through technology and publishing online?
- Have you thought about how students can engage and interact with learning content? Plan opportunities for students to have discussions and ask questions.
- Think about how to make assessments accessible. What reasonable adjustments can be made to assist disabled and dyslexic students?

4. Check

- Communicate with colleagues, especially those who will be teaching on the course. Work together to ensure that your course is accessible. University staff in LeTS (Learning and Teaching Services), Disability and Dyslexia Support Service, CiCS (Corporate Information and Computing Service) and the Student Services Department will be more than happy to assist.

Who benefits from accessible planning?

- Planning to be accessible will save you time and allow students to focus on enjoying the learning process. Happy students will leave good feedback in the National Student Survey; feedback that will positively reflect back on you and the university as a whole.

  The Open University has produced a good introduction to the principles of 'Universal Design' for learning.
  See: www.open.ac.uk/inclusiveteaching/pages/inclusive-teaching/universal-design-for-learning.php

The 'EMPTY VESSEL' theory of learning

Exploring diversity issues

Name: Tomasz

Students aren't all the same. We come from many different countries and backgrounds. Please think about this before teaching a module.

Where you can, please use examples that are relevant to us.

Consider teaching about diversity issues (where relevant) by using a range of examples.

How diverse is the University of Sheffield?

The University of Sheffield is an increasingly diverse community of individuals, each with different needs and experiences. Embracing diversity will provide a richer learning experience for all our students and enable them to graduate with the abilities they need to succeed in the world.

In 2008/9 The University of Sheffield consisted of a student population of 24,319.

- 21% of this population were Non-EU international students.
- 11% of full-time students were aged between 25 and 59 years old.
- The male:female ratio of students was 48:52.
- The University of Sheffield has students from 125 countries.

How can I adapt my teaching to meet the needs of a diverse community?

- Use examples that students of different geo-cultural backgrounds can relate to.
- Consider how your course can be adapted to enable your students to be more globally and culturally aware.
- Design lectures, handouts, assessments and online content to be accessible.

University 'diversity' projects

- **Internationalisation**
  LeTS has produced an excellent resource base that enables academics to explore and contribute ideas about internationalisation:
  www.sheffield.ac.uk/lets/thinkglobal
- **The Sheffield Graduate**
  A useful framework setting out the attributes that enable our students to get the most out of their time with us, ensuring that they are ready for further study, employment and engagement with the wider world:
  www.sheffield.ac.uk/sheffieldgraduate/
- **The University of Sheffield Equality and Diversity pages:**
  www.sheffield.ac.uk/equalityanddiversity/

External Diversity Resources

- Bournemouth University explores the qualities, knowledge and values of a student with a 'global perspective': www.bournemouth.ac.uk/about/the_global_dimension/global_perspectives/global_perspectives.html
- Oxford Brookes University has compiled a range of resources on internationalisation:
  www.brookes.ac.uk/services/ocsld/ioc/resourcekit.html

Hints and tips: Getting started

As a starting point, below is a summary of the central themes and principles that underpin the hints and tips in this chapter. Small changes really do make a difference to your students!

- Handouts, presentations, and assessments shouldn't just be written or expressed clearly, they should be organised clearly. This means using readable fonts, uncluttered text, the correct colours and clear diagrams and images.
- Students respond positively to personal engagement. Get to know them and make yourself available to them. Make students aware that you know who they are.
- Explain the processes and structures of assessment and feedback. Don't simply assume that a student knows what a 2:1 means.
- Digital and web technologies offer a wealth of new potentials in learning and teaching. If you are lacking confidence in these areas, there exist mechanisms of support throughout the University (CICS, LeTS) that can help to get you started.
- Reflect on your teaching practice and strategies.
  How inclusive is your teaching? What knowledge and experience do you expect from your students?

Small changes really do make a difference to your students!

3

Case studies

Academic departments from across the University of Sheffield worked with the Inclusive Learning and Teaching Project. Included here are summaries of a diverse range of contributions: from an arts and community project in the School of English; to the integration of screencasting and podcasting initiatives in the School of Law; to the development of a supportive community for students within the Department of Sociology: no two approaches are the same.

In keeping with the ethos of the project, academic champions worked with their departments to identify the specific areas in which structures and practice could and should be made more inclusive. In almost every case, student participation was central in guiding the department-led projects, first highlighting the need for changes then taking an active role in their delivery.

We hope that these case studies will inspire you to consider Inclusive Learning and Teaching as a necessary concept that can be applied to numerous learning environments. Each example highlights the processes of conceptualisation and delivery as well as critical reflection, which are crucial in the pursuit of effective learning and teaching practice.

The Case studies overview:

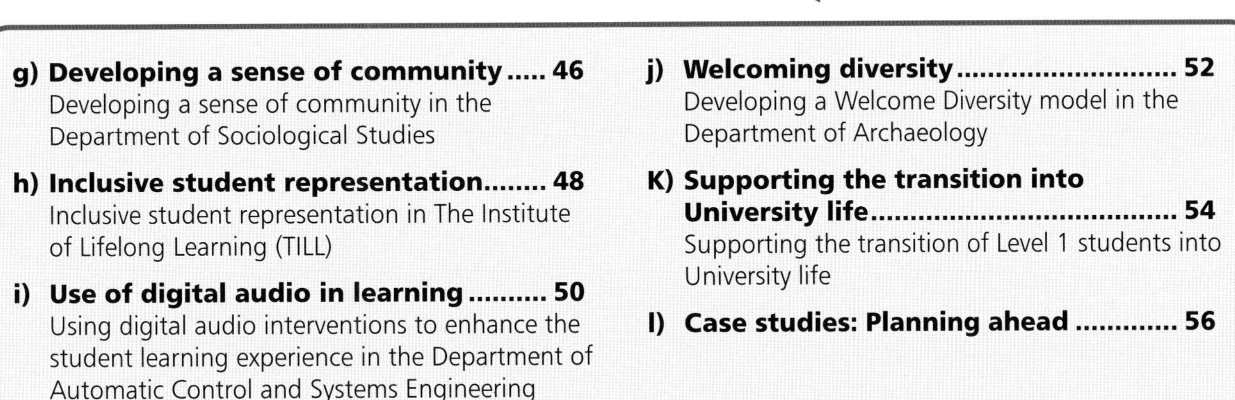

So... everything OK?
oh yes, thanks

Learning with people from the community

Storying Sheffield: setting up a new module in which UG students work alongside people from the city to produce narratives about Sheffield life and their experiences.

Brendan Stone (School of English) and Juliet Storey (Learning and Teaching Services)

What's the issue?

The School of English recognises that the lack of social diversity among its student body (students are predominantly white, female and middle class) may have an impact on students' learning and their preparation for life beyond the University. It also feels that this might discourage people from more diverse backgrounds from applying to study at the School.

What happened next?

Undergraduate students began a module in which they worked alongside people who have tended to be socially excluded and whose voices are less likely to be heard and studied. This year, the 'non-undergraduates' have been long-term users of mental health services. The University waived their fees and they were registered as students for the duration of the course.

There were 32 students studying on the module: 17 short course (external participants) and 15 long-course (undergraduates). Initial sessions covered many areas: narrative as a research method; listening skills; representing life stories using creative means; using images to represent narrative; telling stories through objects; and the history of the imagination. These sessions were led by a wide variety of speakers from within the University, providing short-course and long-course students with the same academic input.

After this, both sets of students worked together to produce works of narrative drawn from the lives and imaginations of the external participants. Outside of the seminars, the undergraduate students organised and promoted an exhibition at which the creative work was showcased and the short-course students received their university certificates. www.storyingsheffield.com has been set up to tell the story of the module and to host students' work.

What did the students say after the project?

Short course students:

"It's helped me to start to mix again."

"This experience has given me the confidence to do a counselling course."

"University gives young people confidence and a bit of that confidence has rubbed off on us."

"Gets you out of a rut of being down – helps you to realise that creative aspects exist in you."

"Made me think differently and look at Sheffield differently."

"Having a student card was another boost to your confidence; a feather in your cap."

"Storying Sheffield has given me the confidence to apply for jobs and I have been successful. I start my new job three days after the exhibition. It's been six years since I last worked."

Long course students:

"We value the opportunity to study in a very different way from the majority of other modules – in particular, the creative and group work aspects of the module."

"This course really allows you to think without limitations creatively…you're not told off for the way you think, you're praised for it."

"The course has removed some of the stigma about mental health for me. It helped me to realise that they are people just like anyone else."

"We developed skills that make us more employable, especially putting on the exhibition. We can show that we are organised, can think for ourselves and can lead a group."

"Working with people from very different backgrounds from ourselves and with very different experiences to our own, was a challenging but valuable learning experience."

What can we learn?

- It is crucial to consult colleagues in a variety of academic and professional areas, particularly in mental health services.
- It is difficult logistically to register students on short courses. Make sure a procedure is in place.
- There should be a role for a Key Worker, who has a pre-existing relationship with the service-users on the course, in order to provide support and expertise.
- Undergraduate students should feel prepared for the unstructured approach to the course. They need the right level of guidance at the outset to ensure that they can approach their work creatively while being reassured that they are on the right track.

b

Enhancing inclusive polices and practice

Identifying ways to enhance the inclusivity of policies and practice in the School of Education.

Terry Lamb, Michelle Moore (Educational Studies) and Andrea Bath (Learning and Teaching Services)

What's the issue?

There are examples of good practice in some programmes relating to inclusion of disabled students, these could be shared across the School. We wanted to gather evidence from past students to provide a basis on which to identify gaps and areas for improvement in the School's policies and practice.

In addition, the School offers a Foundation Degree programme, in Working with Communities, which attracts students from a different sector of the population – many of whom experience financial barriers to study. We wanted to understand the types of support that these students access, and what other areas of assistance might be beneficial to enable them to complete their studies and progress to the BA Honours Degree.

What happened next?

The first strand explored the experience of PGCE students who had a declared disability from the point of application through to entering the workplace. Between March and May 2009, researchers interviewed students from the past three years and the results were collated and analysed.

The second strand looked at issues and financial barriers to study amongst students on the Working with Communities Foundation Degree, using an on-line survey for the current cohort of Year 1 and Year 2 students. Students were asked to indicate the type(s) of issues that affect them during their studies, such as unemployment, redundancy, low income, childcare costs, funding problems and ill health. The survey also explored what type of support they access, who helps them, what additional support might help and whether there were barriers to the continuation of their studies.

The findings from both projects were shared with the School, alongside some suggestions – made by students – for the enhancement of the students' experience.

What did the students say?

PGCE students:

"I didn't know whether to disclose my disability at the application stage."

"My dyslexia makes it difficult for me to express myself during group work, and when I'm writing on the board on placement."

"Before I applied, it was really helpful when a member of staff gave me specific advice about getting experience in different schools."

"It was good to get an information sheet that gave a clear breakdown of what to expect."

"When I applied for jobs the support was brilliant."

Working with Communities Foundation Degree students:

"We want to know what support is available and how to access it, both financially and for the course."

"I would like to stay on for a BA course, but finances will be difficult."

"I'm not sure I'd be able to balance a BA with my job."

"I've got children at home, and childcare costs a lot."

What can we learn?

- Departmental staff time and support time is vital – without the funding we would not be able to collect the interview data.
- Dyslexic students feel that peers and some staff in partner schools poorly understood their disability.
- Financial issues are the main challenge for students on the Working with Communities Foundation Degree and this impacts on their likelihood to continue with their academic studies.

C

Developing inclusive practice guides

Developing simple, readily accessible best practice guides on inclusive learning and teaching and updating departmental information on student support in the School of Law.

Carolyn Shelbourn (School of Law) and Angela Marron (Learning and Teaching Services)

What's this issue?

The way in which teaching material is communicated to students is an obvious area for development. Most teaching materials are available online via MOLE but in many cases they are in limited formats, for example, online handouts or publications. Using podcasts and screencasts to add to the range of teaching methods would allow students to choose how they access the material. This approach would benefit all students by raising accessibility and taking into account individual learning styles.

The School of Law decided to review its methods of teaching delivery as well as its student support mechanisms to ensure that they are as inclusive as possible and in line with best practice for the sector.

What happened next?

An audit was carried out to establish what learning and teaching methods were already being used and how much academic staff knew about the subject.

The project team then set about researching the inclusive teaching strategies in other Russell Group universities, with the Open University being identified for its comprehensive and sympathetic treatment of the subject. Details of the relevant links to the Open University website were included in the material made available to the School of Law.

Material was made available in both electronic and hard copy format and it was agreed that three booklets should be produced for distribution to teaching staff, on the subjects of inclusive learning and teaching methods; podcasting; and screencasting.

Members of staff in the School were briefed on the use of screencasting and podcasting by Dr Kate Campbell-Pilling (School of Law) and Dr Graham McElearney (Learning and Teaching Services). The staff were impressed by the relatively easy means of integrating and deploying these methods into their teaching, and identified numerous benefits for their students' learning, particularly on issues of clarification and revision.

Dr Adrian Powell (Learning and Teaching Services) then led a demonstration of a new software system, Echo360, which captures a lecture at the time of delivery and makes it available in a number of formats. Students can either watch or listen to the lecture again in conjunction with any PowerPoint slides, or they can download it as a podcast.

What did the students say?

"I find screencasts really useful for reminding myself of key points from lectures."

"Podcasts are an accessible and engaging way of learning."

"Using these methods is really helpful for revision during the exam period."

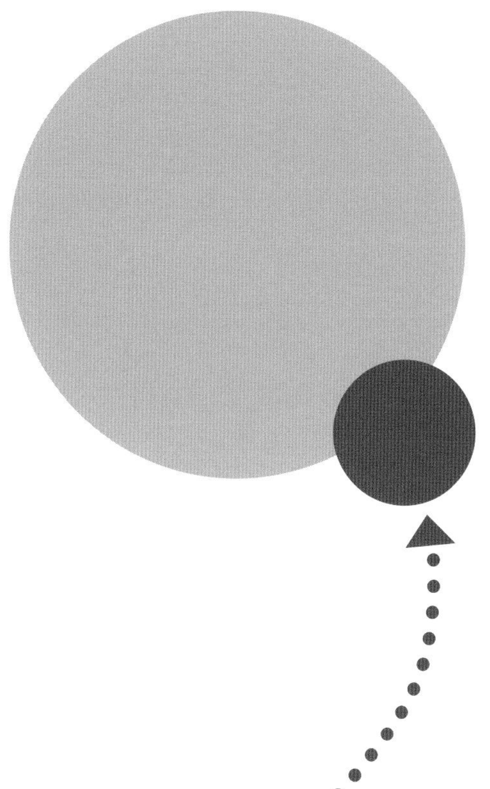

What can we learn?

- The Inclusive Learning and Teaching Project is a benefit to all students, not just those with disabilities.
- Be prepared to encounter opposition if trying to change the established teaching methods.
- Be flexible and realistic about what you are trying to achieve.
- Bringing together academic, technical and support staff allows for a collaborative exchange of skills.
- Web 2.0 has many benefits for learning and teaching; it is important to keep up with the latest developments in technology.
- The greater the variety of teaching methods, the more inclusive teaching becomes.

More Information:

www.sheffield.ac.uk/letspodcast

d

Introducing learning and thinking styles

Introducing learning and thinking styles to new students in the Department of Materials Engineering.

Plato Kapranos (Department of Materials Engineering), Claire Allam and Jane Spooner (Learning and Teaching Services)

What's the issue?

Students arrive at university with vastly differing educational experiences and we need to take a more pro-active stance in managing the transition. We need to help students to settle in by being clear about what is expected of them. A key strategy is to get students to engage with the idea of taking responsibility for their own learning, offering them a range of means to develop their study skills.

What did the students say?

"We want to see our needs and concerns reflected."

What happened next?

Plato Kapranos, a lecturer in the Department of Materials Engineering, had been offering a questionnaire to students on his modules to help them discover their learning and thinking styles. However, many of the students who took part were already in Level 3 and he wanted to introduce the concept to students at the start of their university career and extend the questionnaire across the Department.

The Inclusive Learning and Teaching Project held a focus group for students who had already completed the questionnaire. They confirmed that it was beneficial and offered more points of interest. After the consultation, it was suggested to academic staff in the Department that there should be a session on learning and teaching styles for all incoming students during the induction period.

Plato led a short session during Induction Week which introduced key ideas and then followed up with a longer session during the Department's Study Skills Week, later in Semester 1.

What did the students say after the project?

"We would like to test these ideas with 'hands on' activities."

"It's good to have 'learning and thinking styles' included in Skills Week."

What can we learn?

- Students need support during the transition from school to university; they need guidance in the ways that they can take responsibility for their own learning.
- It's important that students are able to perceive the connections and the value to be derived from this exercise.
- Students thrive on being involved in their own education.
- Students welcome being consulted about their education.
- An active dialogue about learning and teaching between staff and students can help to avoid misunderstandings and create common aims.

More information:

www.sheffield.ac.uk/lets/projects/inclusivel&t/learningstyles.html

Closing the feedback loop

A student-led project in the Department of Mechanical Engineering.

Jenny Rowson (Department of Mechanical Engineering), Henry Brunskill (Student – Department of Mechanical Engineering) and Elena Rodriguez Falcon (Director, Inclusive Learning and Teaching Project)

What's the issue?

The biggest danger in asking students for feedback is not doing anything with it, or doing something but not communicating the actions back to the students. The Department of Mechanical Engineering has traditionally looked for ways to close the feedback loop i.e. email students the actions taken, etc. However, students often feel removed from the process and therefore disinclined to speak out, believing that nothing can be done. The value of feedback must be that it affects change or reflection, therefore when we, as a department, ask for feedback we must be seen to be acting upon it.

What did the students say?

"We value knowing what actions have been taken in response to our feedback and if no action has been taken we want to know what the reasons are."

What happened next?

Henry Brunskill, a final year MEng student, initiated a student forum, with the aim of capturing students' feedback to enhance the inclusive learning and teaching environment in the Department. Students were invited to drop in to the forum and leave any comments they had. The forum captured the thoughts of over 70 students in a period of two hours, with a total of over 120 comments. The comments were written up and divided between inclusive learning and teaching issues and curriculum issues, and were distributed to the relevant committees. Actions taken were communicated back to students.

Under the leadership of Dr Jen Rowson, and in partnership with the students, some 'spin-out' activities emerged. Class shout-outs took place regularly where student representatives encouraged their peers to provide feedback to the Department, and in turn, let the students know the responses. Staff were also encouraged to close the feedback loop by publically communicating any actions to students on the Department's plasma screen and during lectures.

What can we learn?

- Closing the feedback loop increases dialogue between students and the department, enabling more students to come forward to help improve their learning experience.
- Having a student working on a project of this nature from the start – like Henry Brunskill – shows the power of the student voice and enhances engagement.
- Students thrive on being involved in their own education.
- Creating an active dialogue about learning and teaching between staff and students can help to avoid misunderstanding and can create common aims.

f

Involving students: Creating a sense of belonging

Community and involvement of students from the School of Nursing and Midwifery.

Mark Limb (School of Nursing and Midwifery) and Angela Gascoyne (Learning and Teaching Services)

What's the issue?

The School of Nursing and Midwifery wanted to learn more about its students' relationships with the University and their perceptions of what it has to offer. The School's students aren't typical of the University; many of them are in work, often in mid-career. As a result, the modes of study are part-time or continuing professional development. In addition, the School is located in a non-central position. Naturally, these factors may contribute to a feeling of exclusion for Nursing and Midwifery students. With this in mind, the School wanted to know what their students' expectations are, and whether a better sense of community could be developed within the School and with the University.

What did the students say?

"We don't see ourselves as 'typical' students."

"We feel remote from the rest of the University. It feels like the University facilities and information are for full-time, main-campus students."

"If our feedback is having an impact we will get more involved."

"We would be interested in participating in discussions about how the School is governed."

"A web resource – with information about our courses and the support that is available – would be very useful."

What happened next?

Focus groups were set up with two different sets of students. They looked to find out what students wanted from their time at Sheffield and tried to identify barriers to student participation in the School and, more broadly, within the governance of the Faculty. The outcomes were collated and the School considered possible action points.

Web provision was developed to enable part-time and/or distance learning students to engage with student representation and governance activities. Further student consultations took place to develop the resource.

The resource holds key information and contacts and has a uSpace page specifically for part-time students, incorporating agendas and minutes from key committees in the School, and discussion threads and feedback on topics important to the students. These components are adaptable and can be developed and enhanced to meet new challenges.

What can we learn?

- Different types of students need different support.
- Assumptions should not be made about what students deem as important or see as issues.
- Students welcome being consulted about their education and being actively involved in shaping their learning experiences.
- The University still has work has to do in communicating to students how it operates and how they can be involved.

g

Developing a sense of community

Developing a sense of community in the Department of Sociological Studies.

David Phillips, Kevin Farnsworth (Department of Sociological Studies) and Sue Davison (Learning and Teaching Services)

What's the issue?

As part of a broader drive to improve the quality of the learning experience for its students, the Department sees the need to develop an understanding of what makes students feel part of a community. Building on changes already undertaken, it is identified that one of the ways in which this community can be developed is through the integration of more contact time for Level 1 students through seminars.

What happened next?

Focus groups were initiated in order to identify required changes and recognise the success of existing examples of good practice.

The respondents were engaged on a number of issues: induction; contact time; personal support and dissertation supervision; student mentors; learning and teaching and assessment methods; greater challenges in Level 1; a sense of community; changes already undertaken within the Department. The responses to these areas were crucial in informing the Department's approach to inclusion.

What did the students say?

"Registration wasn't a good introduction to University life. It was a very busy time and we had to queue for hours."

"I know that a mentoring system exists, but I'm not sure what it is supposed do."

"We want to be challenged in Level 1. Sometimes we do less work than at A level."

"More can be done to create community; I didn't know we had a common room."

"We want seminar absences to be followed up by the department, so that everyone contributes."

"As a Level 1 student, I was really impressed with how welcome the department made me feel in induction week. It was really important to meet Level 2 and 3 students, too."

"Seminars are really important, we want more of them. They make us feel like we belong in the department – we can get to know each other, and they really help us to clarify the work that is discussed in lectures."

"It really helped that I was encouraged to meet my personal tutor early on."

What can we learn?

- Seminars can be increased to foster a sense of community from staff to students.
- Inductions are important; using them to encourage community between levels 1, 2 and 3 students can be really beneficial.
- Student mentors can be crucial in smoothing the transition to University life, but connections must be made early and frequently.
- Learning and teaching methods can be deployed to get students working together and develop community in academic interactions.
- Student ambassadors can be created to work on induction and 'welcome' activities; encouraging peer-to-peer support and engendering community from the outset.
- Postgraduates can play a key role in supporting undergraduate students.
- Personal tutors should contact students as soon as possible prior to intro week.
- Personal tutors should set out their role early on, and let their students know what they can offer.
- Personal tutors can encourage their students to meet each other, holding small sessions to encourage social and communal aspects of induction.

Inclusive student representation

Inclusive student representation in The Institute of Lifelong Learning (TILL).

Tim Herrick, Darren Webb (The Institute of Lifelong Learning) and Simon Beecroft (Learning and Teaching Services)

What's the issue?

TILL supports the learning of a very diverse cohort of students, all of whom study on a part-time basis. In nearly all cases, students accommodate their studies around a variety of other 'outside' commitments, primarily work and family responsibilities. This limits their ability to engage in University-based extra-curricular events, including representation activities.

For a number of years TILL held a Student Forum which was staff-led and met four times an academic year. However, this did not provide an effective way of gaining representative student views on learning and teaching issues, largely due to poor attendance. In an attempt to make systems of student representation more inclusive, this project sought to learn from students what kinds of representative structure they wanted; develop appropriate mechanisms in response; and enhance the ways in which TILL students engage with the department. It was also hoped that the project would re-engage students with faculty- and university-wide systems of representation, and clarify the important role they had in making visible the diversity of the student body.

What happened next?

The first step was to consult with students and staff to determine what systems of representation would suit them best. Staff from TILL and LeTS ran an online questionnaire and a student focus group, inquiring into attitudes towards and awareness of current systems of representation.

Based on findings from these activities, the face-to-face system of Student Fora was revised and an online environment for staff-student communication was introduced. The new Student Forum met twice an academic year, and had a set agenda. The meetings ran in the early evening and were catered, enabling students to come directly from work, and/or on their way to TILL classes. Detailed notes were taken and circulated by members of staff; action points were identified, followed up, and resultant actions made public.

Alongside this, a new online system of staff-student communication was developed. This was hosted in uSpace, and offered opportunities for students to represent their interests at a time and place of their own choosing. Pre- and post-meeting information was hosted on the uSpace group, which was also used by the Union Link and other student representatives to share information about their work.

Both face-to-face and online activities were staff-student collaborations. Two student ambassadors were engaged to develop the online space and to promote both the online space and the face-to-face meetings. The latter involved visiting a large number of TILL classes to talk about the Student Forum and encourage participation; and both these roles ensured that the Student Forum was seen as something owned by, and relevant to, TILL students.

What can we learn?

- A consultative, inclusive approach to student representation makes for mutually beneficial and effective outcomes.
- The importance of student representation must be made clear before attempting to engage the student voice.
- A good relationship with the Union of Students and an active Union Link are important in building effective channels of student representation.
- Student ambassadors are crucial in the development of a sense of shared ownership.
- For busy adult students the main issue remains one of time. It is crucial to facilitate engagement for time-pressurised students.

i

Use of digital audio in learning

Using digital audio interventions to enhance the student learning experience in the Department of Automatic Control and Systems Engineering.

Anthony Rossiter (Department of Automatic Control and Systems Engineering) and Alison Griffin (Learning and Teaching Services)

What's the issue?

The use of digital audio recorders is widespread amongst students with learning disabilities or with English as an additional language. By enabling the use of recorders for all students the learning experience can be enhanced. It's also important to see how student generated audio can be embedded into the curriculum and to explore what benefits that can bring.

What happened next?

This project temporarily extended the provision of recorders to all Level One students, encouraging the use of the devices to allow students to support, enhance and personalise their learning. Students were encouraged to play back and listen to recordings of all learning interactions, enabling them to reflect; refresh their memories; re-engage their thoughts; and deepen their level of learning.

Students decided for themselves which situations they recorded and how they used their recordings to benefit their experiences. This led to the creation of an online resource that made students aware of the full range of possibilities to enhance their learning, as identified by their peers in focus groups.

What did the students say?

"At university, you need to take responsibility for your own learning and so you need to find out what works best for you."

"We can tailor the use of the recordings for our own needs."

"When a tutor gives me advice on the way to approach an assessment, I can record it and share the information with my course mates."

"I can listen back to lectures at my own pace. As a student with English as an additional language, this is very helpful."

"If I misunderstand things I can listen back to my recordings for clarification, rather than immediately having to ask the tutor."

"There was a time when I thought I had lost it and felt like some part of myself was missing because I was so used to using it. When I found it I was really happy."

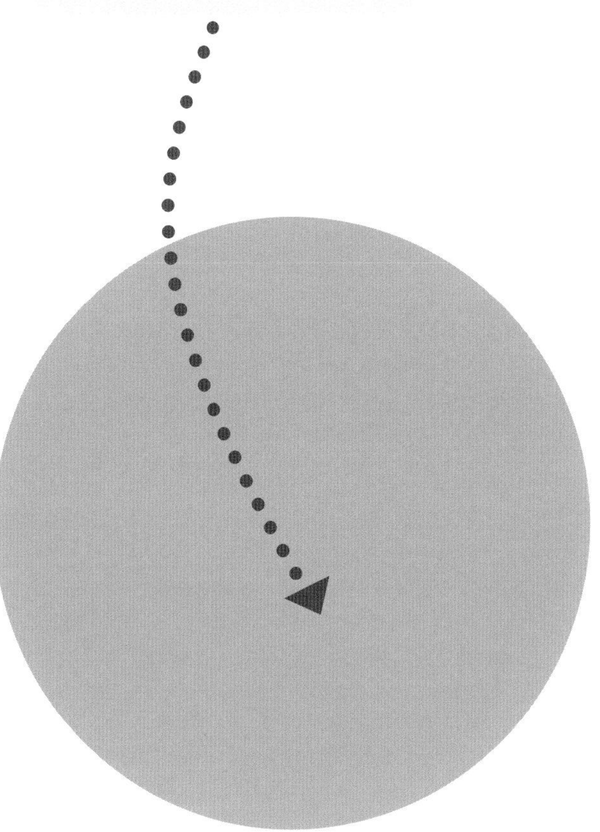

What can we learn?

- Ensure recorders are available from the beginning of Semester 1 so students can start to use them from the outset and they become an integrated part of learning in the department.
- In a situation where many students are likely to be recording, e.g., guest lectures, consider producing a single recording available to all students via MOLE.
- Students recognised that this was a tool to supplement and enhance their learning and planned to download visual learning resources such as lecture notes and slides to complement their recordings.
- Because of the frequent use of equations and symbols in calculations, students emphasised the importance of visual learning, so audio recordings were not always helpful.
- Students were clear that recording lectures was not a substitute for note taking as they would still take notes when listening back to lectures. In fact, students emphasised that note taking would become more focussed and targeted than in a lecture situation where students tended to write *everything down*.
- Taking notes retrospectively allowed students to consider the entirety of the lecture first.

j

Welcoming diversity

Developing a Welcome Diversity model in the Department of Archaeology.

Glynis Jones, Bob Johnston (Department of Archaeology) and James Goldingay (Learning and Teaching Services)

What's the issue?

A relatively large number of students enter their degree programmes through non-standard routes and therefore they have non-traditional requirements. The department operates a flexible approach to students taking leave of absence and entering at non-standard entry points, it is felt that the induction of these students on their return would benefit from further attention. Induction for the relatively high number of mature students and Erasmus entrants also deserves special attention. While there is not a perceived problem with any particular area in the Department, there is a degree of uncertainty over the support levels for certain student groupings. It is also felt that the standard Level 1 personal and academic tutorial system would benefit from a similar review.

What happened next?

A project was conceived to develop a Welcome Diversity model for the Department of Archaeology. There was an emphasis on using induction to welcome students who may have a diverse range of needs and requirements, e.g. students who are returning from leave of absence, part-time students from the Institute of Lifelong Learning, students transferring from other institutions, mature students, students for whom English is not their first language and students with disabilities, as well as standard entry students at Level 1. Student opinion was canvassed through questionnaires, focus groups and interviews, to identify and engage the student voice. This was done in order to extend the scope of the project and to ensure that the Department's Welcome Diversity model therefore caters for incoming students from all backgrounds and levels of entry.

What did the students say?

Level 1 tutorial system students:

"If I'm having difficulties I'll contact the Department first; the staff and tutors are approachable."

"We like having regular tutor meetings and learning in small groups."

"If I'm having difficulties I'll contact the Department first; the staff and tutors are approachable."

Erasmus/Year Abroad and non-standard entry and mature students:

"I'm part-time, so my tutor having flexible office hours is really important."

"I really appreciate the personal tutorial system, and it's good that as a mature student, a specific member of staff looks after our interests."

"It's so useful being able to do more core reading through online resources, it would be great to have more digital resources."

"As an Erasmus student, it's really good to be consulted on modules even though we don't register until we arrive back; it shows the department is thinking of our needs and requirements."

Diversity in the coffee place

What can we learn?

- Tutorials should be closely integrated into the curriculum of the module, specifically linking the topics covered in lectures with the tutorials and essays.
- Keep Erasmus/Year Abroad students 'in the loop' on module choices and registration when they are away from the University.
- 'Welcome' is vital for enabling students to feel relaxed and well informed about their learning. This does not only apply to Level 1 students, but those who may be returning from a year abroad, a leave of absence, joining from another institution, or from non-traditional backgrounds.
- Structures should be developed so that when mature/part-time students have an issue, there is appropriate tutorial provision.
- A 'welcome pack' could be devised for returning students, and students entering the department at a level other than Level 1.
- The Departmental website would benefit from a revamp, with particular attention paid to the Erasmus/Year Abroad pages.

k

Supporting the transition into University life

Supporting the transition of Level 1 students into university life.

David Mowbray (Department of Physics and Astronomy) and Alison Griffin, Marie Evans (Learning and Teaching Services)

What's the issue?

In 2008, the Department of Physics and Astronomy undertook a review of its First Year curriculum. This was driven by a number of factors including a dramatic increase in student numbers and recognition, within the Department, that the Physics knowledge base amongst new undergraduates had become narrower.

The Department wanted to enhance its understanding of what new Level 1 students might expect, want and need from their experience at the University of Sheffield so that it could best support them as they moved from school/college into higher education.

What happened next?

Staff from Physics and LeTS (Learning and Teaching Services) ran a focus group for new Level one students. A focus group was also held for Level 2 students so that the views of students, once they were able to reflect on their experience of Level 1, were available to the Department. Both groups explored the same issues: induction, teaching and learning, academic support, personal support, exams and general reflection on their overall experience.

Semester 1 exams were a recurrent theme identified by the focus groups and so this was explored further via a short on-line questionnaire distributed to all Level 1 students. A third of students responded.

The outcomes of this research (the focus groups plus questionnaire) were then considered by the Head of Department/Director of Teaching and discussed at an away-day of the Department's Teaching Committees. A number of changes have been made to departmental practice in light of this work, for example, the Department has increased formative assessment by introducing an on-line assessment tool at Level 1.

What can we learn?

- Addressing an issue which has been identified as a priority for a department ensures resources are available to produce effective results.
- Talking to students and listening to what they have to say provides a very useful way of:
  - developing an more in-depth understanding of issues identified through student evaluation questionnaires
  - confirming/challenging staff perceptions.
- Support from a senior level (in this case the Head of Department) results in real change.

Case studies: Planning ahead

The list below summarises some key learning points drawn from the case studies. These reflections are intended to build an instructive platform for the development of your own projects and initiatives.

- When altering existing modules radically, or creating new ones, it is important to keep students reassured and to make sure that they are comfortable with the pace and processes of change.
- Be flexible and realistic and don't do it all on your own. The case studies show the importance of partnerships between academic and support staff; don't be afraid to ask for help.
- It is important to consider students as individuals; be mindful of different learning styles and educational and cultural backgrounds. Good Inclusive practice can be generated by deploying a *variety* of methods drawn from an understanding of an equally diverse student body.
- Students welcome involvement and consultation; allow them to realise that they can actively shape their educational experiences and that they will be rewarded if they engage in this manner.

What is needed for a successful project?

Typically, a departmental project requires support from senior management, for example, the Heads of Department, to legitimise the work, 'doers' to identify the issue and drive the work forward and students to offer their perspective and practical support.

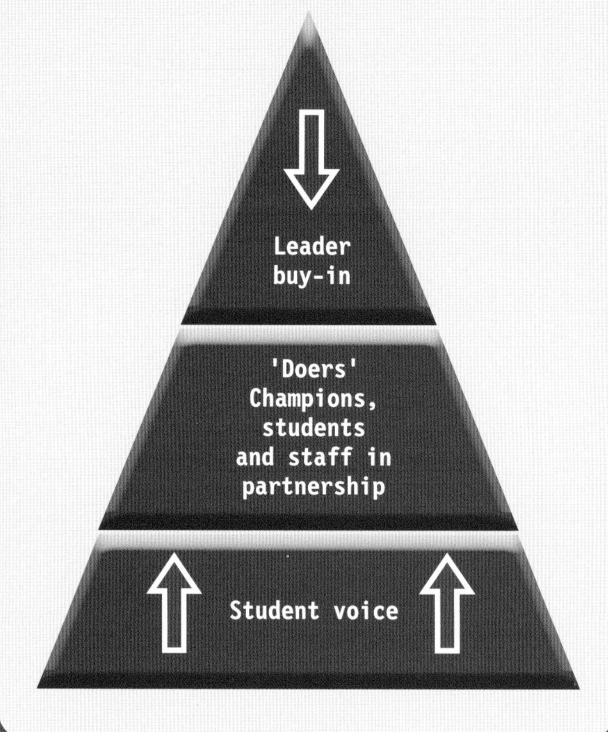

Student engagement and partnership

This section is designed to both reflect the role and influence of the students in the ILT Project and to show – from their perspective – the benefits of empowering students in the pursuit of inclusive practice.

It summarises the research undertaken by Emily Savage. As the Students' Union Education Officer (2007–2008), Emily played a vital role in getting students involved in the Project. She was subsequently commissioned by the Project to research the importance of student engagement and the empowerment of the student voice.

Getting started

If the Project was to have long-term impact it was vital that the initiative came from the students, and that the University had to be reactive and open-minded in its partnership with them. The Project's work on initiating and developing student ownership has attempted to embed principles of reflection, co-operation and action, altering the dynamic between students and the University. To deliver this, the Inclusive Learning and Teaching Project worked with students as partners, they weren't used in order to legitimise its practices and activities, they got involved actively and equally to dictate real change.

The Students' Union was an early point of contact for the Project, energising students with the unique nature of the Project. Specifically, the Students' Union Officers saw the University reaching out to the Union, not on a consultative basis, but with the hope of a engendering a mutually enriching relationship that had the potential to change the way students engaged in their learning experiences. This partnership began to draw in students who were passionate about inclusion, many of whom sensed that things were different this time and that the University was willing to both *listen* and act.

Initiating Ownership

Students attended a preliminary 'ideas session' and many were initially sceptical. However, they soon realised that this project was different. For a start, complimentary food and refreshments were made available, a minor point perhaps, but these kinds of touches illustrated the extent to which the University was reaching out and accommodating the students, making them feel that their presence was valued and that their ideas where sought. Moreover, the passion of the project team and their eagerness to develop partnerships with the students quickly established a tone that energised all who were present.

Going into the session, the project team seemed to have no pre-conceived ideas or expectations about what they wanted or expected to hear; the atmosphere was relaxed and open. The meeting never descended into a talking shop where students simply moaned about their lecturers; instead, an environment was facilitated which enabled the student voice to be given coherence and focus. Questions were posed such as: 'What needs to change?' and 'What would inclusive learning and teaching look like?' These kinds of prompts enabled a wide-ranging set of ideas and actions to emerge.

It soon became clear that this wasn't a 'box ticking' exercise, the students involved weren't simply there to rubber-stamp a set of pre-ordained policies, they were recognising the fact that senior academics were *listening* to them and that this was just the start. The early sessions gave rise to a number of initiatives and activities which saw the Project gather momentum quickly: many of the suggestions and ideas found their way into the Project's 'Hints and Tips' calendar; students were given defined roles and responsibilities to drive the Project forward; and students attended faculty meetings and talked about inclusion with heads of

department, opening up new lines of communication and influencing decision makers. Crucially, the Project was identifying the students as co-researchers and colleagues and empowering them to drive forward its principles.

The students – many of whom had previously had unfulfilling experiences of being asked for their opinions and seeing no evidence of change – were for the first time contributing ideas which were engaged with and acted upon promptly and visibly.

The learning process

The Inclusive Learning and Teaching Project's relationship with students inevitably generated a number of learning points. For example, the early sessions were characterised by a productive and exciting energy, but it is now clear that it is crucial for this to be maintained throughout: student ownership is as much about continuity as it is about partnership. It is vital to recognise that students may not be able to consistently perform a long-term role, for example, their degree may alter or their workload might increase, they may have part-time jobs or different pressures at home, or they may, simply, leave university or graduate. The early enthusiasm must be consolidated and built on: students can offer a great deal of time and energy at the start which may not be maintained consistently, it is vital that those students are communicated with and that their input is sought and recognised regularly. Similarly, a broader range of students should be engaged, in order to reduce the potential for an over-concentration of student input in one year which may then lead to a subsequent drop in following years: the project must be flexible and responsive to changes in the student dynamic. Indeed, Students' Union officers and representatives have a limited time in their role, it is crucial that the foundations of the project are strong enough to transcend these limitations by appealing to new students and adapting approaches to meet new challenges.

While much of the impetus for student ownership came from an engagement with the Students' Union, it is also important that these kinds of partnerships extend into the wider student body. One of the greatest triumphs of the Project is the way that it has shown that inclusive practices can benefit the learning experiences of the many and not the few, and it is the disenfranchised, silent majority – many of whom will be experiencing positive changes to their learning experiences without even knowing it – who need to be allowed to recognise that they can have a say in their education.

The Inclusive Learning and Teaching Project has shown that it is possible to engage the student voice and initiate symbiotic partnerships between the University and its students, which have the potential to redefine the learning experience for all.

This is just the start. As the top-up fee debate continues, students are become increasingly aware of their own voice. The Inclusive Learning and Teaching Project has shown that this voice need not be feared; that with a little guidance it has the power to articulate and shape positive change.

Tips for student engagement

- Give a small group responsibility for driving the project, or elements of it, forward but ensure that ideas come from a much wider student community.
- Get students out and about around busy spaces in the university, promoting the project to their peers.

- Get module evaluations and questionnaires to ask questions such as 'How could we improve the module?' These kinds of prompts encourage the students to make suggestions and to share their experiences of a particular learning experience in a constructive way.
- Ensure students feel that they are playing a leading role in the project and that student engagement is at the centre. Students need to know that they are being listened to and that they are affecting change directly.
- Make sure students can see the product of their labour. One of the major successes of the Project has been the way that student-generated ideas – first mooted in workshop sessions – were then put into practice both quickly visibly.
- Maintain communication with students throughout the process of engagement.
- Make sure that new students are aware of what you are doing; establish enthusiasm and interest early.
- Illustrate and provide evidence of changes that have been brought about as a result of student engagement.
- Make interactions with students fun and accommodating; a relaxed atmosphere will generate a more productive discussion.

The Student Voice

Bringing about change: Key factors

Bringing about change is challenging.

We have argued that three of the key factors that any project should include are:

- Having top-down support and the leadership of a senior figure.
- Identifying and supporting the 'doers' or 'champions'.
- Enabling the student voice to drive the cause.

We also argued that staff and students working together make the most effective champions.

In the following section, Dr David Forrest (School of English) describes the key factors through which the Inclusive Learning and Teaching Project brought about change, including the importance of critical reflection. He also talks further about engaging students and listening to their voice and he discusses the relevance of building a community of learners.

We must first reflect and then identify.

Critical reflection

Research led teaching might be defined as a critical reflection on the ways knowledge is created, evaluated and applied. The teaching itself might therefore involve the critical assessment of the assumptions we often make about what is best for a student, or a set of students. A central part of our duty as teachers is to identify the skills a student needs and the best way to encourage the adoption of those skills. If the means by which we teach these skills is successful for most of those students, then surely we are doing our jobs well? But what of those who don't fit our assumptions? What of the students whose needs and requirements are different from those of the 'archetypes' that we construct and base our teaching around? Inclusive learning and teaching is about *challenging* our assumptions and *recognising* the need for changes to cater for *all* and not just for the majority of those who we teach.

We know that students learn in different ways: that some respond more effectively to images, others to words, other to sounds, others to movement. We know that the best way to learn is to do and that students as apprentices in the craft of evaluating knowledge will be more successful than students as consumers of what is supposedly established. We know that students' backgrounds differ dramatically: that they come from a wide variety of educational and social environments. We know that some students experience disabilities that present challenges for their participation in their own education, and that it is our duty to ensure that these do not limit their potential to learn and achieve. What the Inclusive Learning and Teaching Project has shown is that small and un-dramatic changes in the learning environment can make a big difference not only for an individual student but for all students.

Recognising and engaging the student voice

The case studies of inclusive learning and teaching practice that form the bulk of this handbook are characterised by a process of critical reflection combined with an engagement of students. It is not for one person to identify the barriers to students' learning experience, nor is it for a group of people; rather, it is for the students themselves to highlight and respond to the issues, before then playing an active role in shaping resolutions.

As academic departments contributed to the Project, the importance of mutual exchanges between staff and students and a privileging of the student voice were key factors in the development and success of strategies in a variety of areas. Case studies; questionnaires; consultations; drop boxes; students attending faculty meetings; the means of engagement were wide and varied, but the principle was consistent: inclusion cannot be achieved without the partnership necessary to enable students to have an equal say and to be listened to.

The PowerPoint format that you have used effectively for the last few years has survived because nobody has told you that it is difficult to read. Then one student draws your attention to the difficulty they have reading the presentation and wonders if you could adapt the text to a larger font size and use different colours. You do so, and apply the changes to all your future presentations. One student's learning experience is made easier in that particular lecture; but you have made a simple alteration that will make your practice more inclusive for years to come.

Listening to the student voice; acting on the student voice.

Building a community

'For me, the most exciting thing in learning and teaching [has been]... the growing recognition that academics and students share a collective interest in meeting the challenges of developing our learning environment to be more accessible for all students. The enthusiasm to meet these challenges has been universal and has led to an explosion of exciting projects that are making significant contributions and really make this year stand apart.'

Richard Kelwick, student

This project has run as a community: many academics, students, support staff and managers have shaped and sustained it. Here at Sheffield, Learning and Teaching Services have facilitated a set of working practices that reflect the communal principles of successful practices: collaboration, communication and co-operation are key. The mutual exchange of support and ideas between students, the academic champion(s) and a supportive Head of Department, have been the markers of success. A recognition of the qualities and resources that each of these elements contribute is essential in developing a model for continued development in Inclusive Learning and Teaching.

That this emphasis on recognition, reflection, and community mirrors the ideal conditions for inclusive teaching and learning as well as research led teaching is no coincidence. This project represents the application to learning and teaching of the principle that has underscored academic endeavour for centuries: that enriching experience in education is not about listening to one voice but is about listening to, sharing and evaluating from as many different voices as possible for the benefit of all.

Creating a learning culture and a learning community for all.

that includes
you!
staff

Afterword: And so, what now?

The only answer we can offer to this question is: now you go and do it!

Every one of us has a responsibility to our students, to our institution, to the community and to ourselves to do whatever it takes to create and develop an environment where all students and staff alike can thrive and achieve. However, there are also less idealistic reasons for having to proactively ensure that our learning and teaching culture is inclusive. For example, it is reasonable to suggest that an increase in fees will mean that students will have higher expectations for their learning experience, and the National Student Survey will, no doubt, continue to reflect students' satisfaction or the lack of it. As Professor Anne Peat (School of Nursing and Midwifery) says: "We cannot afford not to do this".

Sceptics argue that universities in the Russell Group will not suffer from recruitment problems. We say, we don't know that for sure but even if that were the case, we have a duty to recruit a more diverse student population and to enable and prepare them to become the next generation of professionals who will solve the challenges of today's world.

We also know that many Higher Education Institutions are working to develop an inclusive learning and teaching culture, including other Russell Group universities. Most approaches, however, focus on particular groups such as students with disabilities. We argue that our responsibility and therefore, commitment is to ALL students.

Professor John Barrett argues that: "Research led universities have to demonstrate more clearly than most that the teaching of the way knowledge is created, assessed, and applied (which is what he takes research led teaching to be) is accessible to all because it must defend the principle that research led teaching is democratic and not elitist. Any block to a student's ability to access the processes of enquiry and learning is a failure of the institution and not the product of some intellectual mystery yet to be revealed to that student."

There is plenty of evidence to demonstrate the need for cultural change where, if a university does not have an inclusive learning and teaching approach, it is not only unwise but also "unacceptable" as Sarah Shreeve , one of our student champions, said.

The good news is that developing an inclusive learning and teaching experience for your students, for our students, is actually a straightforward thing to do.

- Keep in mind that changes benefit ***all*** students – move from a focus on specific target groups – (mature, international, disabled, etc) to ALL students.
- Have an active dialogue with your students: it promotes understanding and collaboration and it leads to significant enhancement. Involving students also brings energy, enthusiasm and a significant 'voice' that delivers a much more powerful message than any other stakeholder involved could.
- Don't make assumptions about what students need – they are better placed to tell you!
- Ask them, do something about it (in partnership with them if possible) and tell them what you have done. Close the loop!
- In this handbook, we have provided you with case studies and hints and tips that clearly evidence that minor changes can make a big difference. And now it is over to you!

Elena Rodriguez-Falcon
Director of Learning and Teaching Development
Inclusive Learning and Teaching Project

Rare creatures of the Academic Reef Fig. 1

Further reading

Many of the ideas expressed and offered in this handbook have their roots in a wide range of scholarly writing. This section draws together a selection of the academic sources that have proved useful during the course of the project.

General approaches to learning and teaching

- Merriam, S.B. & Associates, (2007) *Non-Western Perspectives On Learning and Knowing* (Florida: Krieger Publishing Company)
- Kapranos, P & Tsakiropoulos, P., (2008) 'Teaching Engineering Students', International Symposium for Engineering Education, Dublin City University, Ireland, September 2008
- Ball, D.L., (2000) 'Bridging Practices: Intertwining Content and Pedagogy in Teaching and Learning to Teach', *Journal of Teacher Education* vol. 51, no. 3 pp. 241–247
- Murray, H.G., Rushton, J.P. & Paunonen, S.V., (1990) 'Teacher Personality Traits and Student Instructional Ratings in Six Types of University Courses', *Journal of Educational Psychology* vol. 82, no. 2 pp. 250–261
- Cuthbert, P.F., (2005) 'The student learning process: Learning styles or learning approaches?', *Teaching in Higher Education* vol. 10, no. 2 pp. 235–249
- Group, A.t.H.E.S, (2004) 'Fair Admissions to Higher Education: Recommendations for Good Practice'. www.admissions-review.org.uk/downloads/finalreport.pdf

Curriculum development

- Kapranos, P, (2008) 'Developments on the delivery of Non-technical modules to Engineering Materials & Bio-engineering students', International Symposium for Engineering Education, Dublin City University, Ireland, September 2008
- Envick, B.R. & Envick, D., (2007) 'Toward a Stakeholder-Focused Curriculum: Examining Specific University Program Offerings against Competencies Provided by the U.S. Department of Labor', *Journal of the Scholarship of Teaching and Learning* vol. 7, no. 2 pp.79–89
- Fraser, S. & Bosanquet, A., (2006) 'The curriculum? That's just a unit outline, isn't it?' *Studies in Higher Education* vol. 31, no 3 pp. 269–284

Critical reflection for students and teachers

- Kapranos, P., (2007) '21st century Teaching & Learning – Kolb Cycle & Reflective Thinking as part of teaching Creativity', International Symposium for Engineering Education, Dublin City University, Ireland, September 2007
- Marsh, H.W., & Roche, L.A., (1997) Making Students' Evaluations of Teaching Effectiveness Effective: The Critical Issues of Validity, Bias, and Utility, *American Psychologist* vol. 52, no. 11 pp. 1187–1197
- Rae, A.M. & Cochrane, D.K., (2008) 'Listening to students: How to make written assessment feedback useful' *Active Learning in Higher Education* vol. 9, no. 3 pp. 217–230

- Chevalier, A., Gibbons, S., Thorpe, A., Snell, M., & Hoskins, S. L., (2009) 'Performance and Perception: Differences in self-assessment between students', *Economics of Education Review* vol. 28, no. 6 pp. 716–727
- Goldstein, G.S. & Benassi, V.A., (2006) 'Students' and Instructors' Beliefs About Excellent Lecturers and Discussion Leaders', *Research in Higher Education* vol 46, no. 6 pp. 685–707

Inclusive practice and theory

- Jackson, S., (2005) 'When Learning comes of Age? Continuing Education into Later Life', *Journal of Adult and Continuing Education* vol. 11, no. 2 pp. 188–199
- Fuller, M., Healey, M., Bradley, A. & Hall, T., (2004) 'Barriers to learning: a systematic study of the experience of disabled students in one university', *Studies in Higher Education* vol. 29, no. 3 pp. 303–318
- Chavez, C.I. & Weisinger, J.Y., (2008) 'Beyond diversity training: A social infusion for cultural inclusion', *Human Resource Management* vol. 47, no. 2 pp. 331–350
- Barrington, E., (2004) 'Teaching to student diversity in higher education: how Multiple Intelligence Theory can help', *Teaching in Higher Education* vol. 9, no. 4 pp. 421–434
- Ainscow, M., (2005) 'Developing inclusive education systems: what are the levers for change?', *Journal of Educational Change* vol. 6, no. 2 pp. 109–124 www.open.ac.uk/inclusiveteaching www.sheffield.ac.uk/lets/inclusive
- Jessop, T., & Williams, A., (2005) 'Equivocal tales about identity, racism and the curriculum', *Teaching in Higher Education* vol. 14, no. 1 pp. 95–106
- Skelton, A., (2002) 'Towards Inclusive Learning Environments in Higher Education? Reflections on a Professional Development Course for University Lecturers', *Teaching in Higher Education* vol. 7, no. 2 pp. 193–214

Widening participation

- Osborne, M., (2003) 'Increasing or Widening Participation in Higher Education? – A European overview', *European Journal of Education* vol. 38, no. 1 pp. 5–24
- Naidoo, R., (2000) 'The 'Third Way' to widening participation and maintaining quality in higher education: lessons from the United Kingdom', *Journal of Educational Enquiry* vol. 1, no. 2 pp. 24–38
- Kettley, N., (2007) 'The past, present and future of widening participation research', *British Journal of Sociology of Education* vol. 28, no. 3 pp. 333 – 347
- Broecke, S. & Nicholls, T., (2007) 'Ethnicity and Degree Attainment; Research Report www.heacademy.ac.uk/assets/York/documents/events/archive/SinghG_Coventry_Race_EqualityNSS_8May08.pdf [Accessed 23rd June 2010]

Using new technologies

- www.sheffield.ac.uk/letspodcast/index.html
- Middleton, A., (2008) 'Audio Feedback: timely media interventions' www.herts.ac.uk/fms/documents/teaching-and-learning/blu/conference2008/Andrew-Middleton-2008.pdf